DATE DUE

PRINTED IN U.S.A.

HOW ARE THEY DIFFERENT?

Tell Me the DIFFERENCE Between a

SEAL and a
SEA LION

Leigh Rockwood

PowerKiDS press
New York

Published in 2013 by The Rosen Publishing Group, Inc.
29 East 21st Street, New York, NY 10010

First Edition

Editor: Joanne Randolph
Book Design: Kate Laczynski

Photo Credits: Cover (seal) Gentoo Multimedia Ltd./Shutterstock.com; cover (sea lion) Craig K. Lorenz/Photo Researchers/Getty Images; p. 4 All Canada Photos RM/Getty Images; p. 5 Antoine Beyeler/Shutterstock. com; p. 6 worldswildlifewonders/Shutterstock.com; p. 7 Bjorn Stefanson/Shutterstock.com; p. 8 Nathalie Michel/The Image Bank/Getty Images; p. 9 Robert HM Voors/Shutterstock.com; p. 10 Danita Delimont/Gallo Images/Getty Images; p. 11 Ryan M. Bolton/Shutterstock.com; p. 12 Dougal Waters/The Image Bank/Getty Images; p. 13 © iStockphoto.com/Diana Amster; p. 14 Pi-Lens/Shutterstock.com; p. 15 Gerard Soury/Oxford Scientific/Getty Images; p. 16 Tory Kallman/Flickr/Getty Images; p. 17 © iStockphoto.com/Linda Mirro; p. 18 Paul Marotta/Flickr/Getty Images; p. 19 Tony Campbell/Shutterstock.com; p. 20 Anneka/Shutterstock.com; p. 21 Stubblefield Photography/Shutterstock.com; p. 22 naturediver/Shutterstock.com.

Library of Congress Cataloging-in-Publication Data

Rockwood, Leigh.
 Tell me the difference between a seal and a sea lion / by Leigh Rockwood. — 1st ed.
     p. cm. — (How are they different?)
Includes index.
ISBN 978-1-4488-9640-0 (library binding) — ISBN 978-1-4488-9738-4 (pbk.) —
ISBN 978-1-4488-9739-1 (6-pack)
1. Seals (Animals)—Juvenile literature. 2. Sea lions—Juvenile literature. I. Title.
QL737.P63R63 2013
599.79—dc23

                    2012023900

Manufactured in the United States of America

CPSIA Compliance Information: Batch #W13PK5: For Further Information contact Rosen Publishing, New York, New York at 1-800-237-9932

CONTENTS

LET'S LOOK AT SEALS AND SEA LIONS

Sea lions and seals look a lot alike and are often mistaken for one another. These marine **mammals** both have barrel-shaped bodies and flippers that help them move through the water. Sea lions and seals belong to a group

Harbor seals are one of the most common kinds of seals. They live along most coasts in the Northern Hemisphere, or half, of the world.

Galápagos sea lions live near the Galápagos Islands. They eat mainly sardines.

of animals called **pinnipeds**. Pinnipeds include sea lions, seals, fur seals, and walruses.

Because sea lions and seals are related, you will need to learn more about them to tell them apart. This book will show you what to look for when trying to identify sea lions and seals.

SEA LIONS, SEALS, AND TRUE SEALS

Elephant seals are one of the 19 species of true seals. These seals get their name from their trunk-like snouts, which they can fill with air to make loud roaring sounds.

Scientists named pinnipeds for their feet. They gave the group a name that comes from the Latin words meaning "winged feet."

The pinnipeds are further grouped into three scientific families. Walruses are one family. A second family contains the 7 sea lion

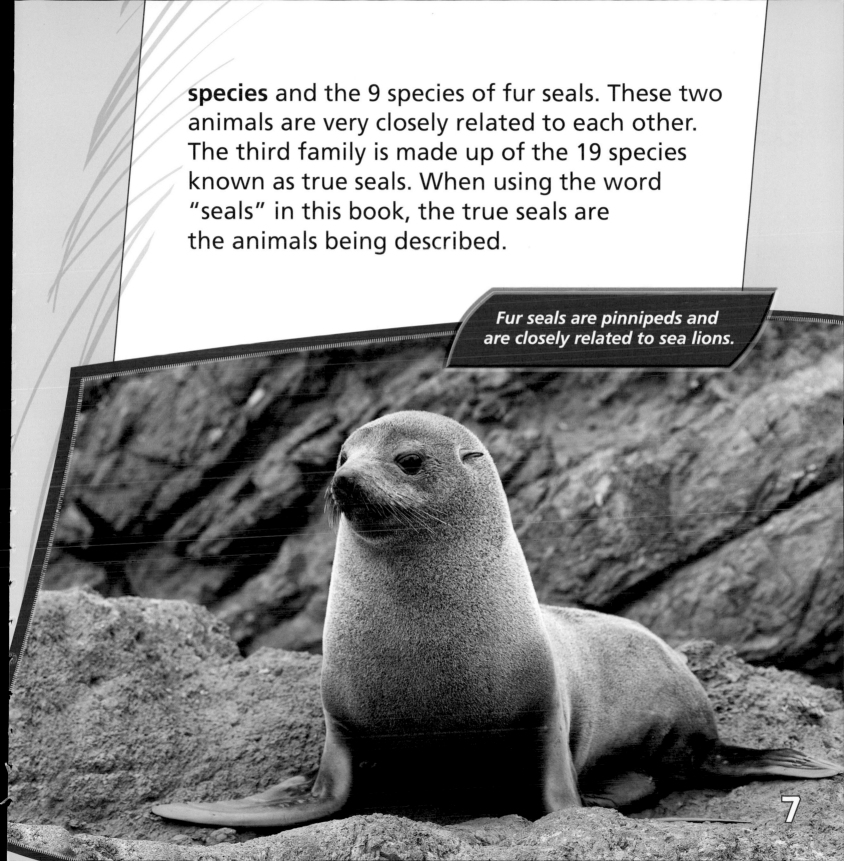

species and the 9 species of fur seals. These two animals are very closely related to each other. The third family is made up of the 19 species known as true seals. When using the word "seals" in this book, the true seals are the animals being described.

Fur seals are pinnipeds and are closely related to sea lions.

HOW ARE SEALS AND SEA LIONS ALIKE?

Sea lions and seals have many things in common. Although both animals may look sleek and hairless from a distance, seals and sea lions have fur, just as other mammals do. As marine mammals, they both have thick layers

Sea lions come ashore when it is time to have babies, as do seals.

Both seals and sea lions can live in very cold places due to their blubber, which keeps them warm.

of fat, called blubber, that keeps them warm in cold ocean water. They also need to come to the top of the water to breathe.

Both animals also have flippers for swimming and spend a great deal of their time in the ocean looking for fish to eat. When it is time to have babies, both sea lions and seals come together onshore or on ice in big, noisy social groups.

EARS OR NO EARS?

Believe it or not, a small but telling difference between seals and sea lions is the ears. If you are looking at a pinniped at the zoo, look at the sides of the animal's head. Do you see little flaps or just holes?

The ear holes on this bearded seal are easy to see.

If you see a small flap on each side of the animal's head, you are looking at the ears of a sea lion. Seals, on the other hand, do not have earflaps. If you are looking at a seal, you will see only a small ear hole on either side of its head.

COMPARING SEALS

SCIENTIFIC FAMILY	Phocidae
NUMBER OF SPECIES	19
FLIPPERS	Small, furry, better for swimming than walking
EARS	Ear holes
DIET	Meat
LARGEST SPECIES	Southern elephant seal, 20 feet (6 m) long and 8,800 pounds (4,000 kg)
MALE/FEMALE	Bull/cow
BABY NAME	Pup

and SEA LIONS

Otariidae	**SCIENTIFIC FAMILY**
7	**NUMBER OF SPECIES**
Large, hairless, can be used for walking on land	**FLIPPERS**
Earflaps	**EARS**
Meat	**DIET**
Steller sea lion, 9.25 feet (2.8 m) long and 2,400 pounds (1,089 kg)	**LARGEST SPECIES**
Bull/cow	**MALE/FEMALE**
Pup	**BABY NAME**

ALL ABOUT FLIPPERS

Another way to tell the difference between sea lions and seals is to look at the animal's flippers and watch how the animal moves. Sea lions are better **adapted** to moving on land. They have larger, stronger front flippers than do seals. In addition, their back flippers can

Sea lions and fur seals can run on all four flippers when on land.

turn around and face forward. This lets sea lions waddle around when they are out of the water.

Seals have powerful back flippers, which help push them through the water. They cannot turn these flippers forward for walking on land, though. Seals also have smaller, weaker front flippers than do sea lions. Because of this, seals can only roll around or drag themselves along the ground.

Seals may be awkward on land, but they are built perfectly for swimming. The flippers are hands and feet that have adapted to act like paddles to pull the animal through the water.

15

FURRY COATS

Seals and sea lions both have layers of blubber and furry coats that **insulate**, or keep their bodies warm. Sea lions tend to have coarse brownish hair with little to no markings. For example, the California sea lion's fur ranges from light brown to almost black. Seals often have short, stiff hair and have a wider range of

Hawaiian monk seals have gray fur on most of their bodies, with lighter fur on their bellies. Monk seals spend much of their time alone, unlike other seals.

California sea lions have brown fur. Males generally have darker fur than do the females.

colors and markings than do sea lions. Leopard seals, for example, are named for their spotted grayish coats.

Each year, seals and sea lions **molt**, or shed their hair. Sea lions molt gradually, so they are insulated enough to enter the ocean while molting. Seals molt all at once and must fast and stay on land until their new coats come in!

This colony of seals has hauled out of the water on the shores of Cape Cod, Massachusetts.

Seals and sea lions are **semiaquatic** marine mammals. This means that while they spend most of their time in the ocean, they need to come onto land or ice sometimes. For this reason, these pinnipeds are found in coastal areas.

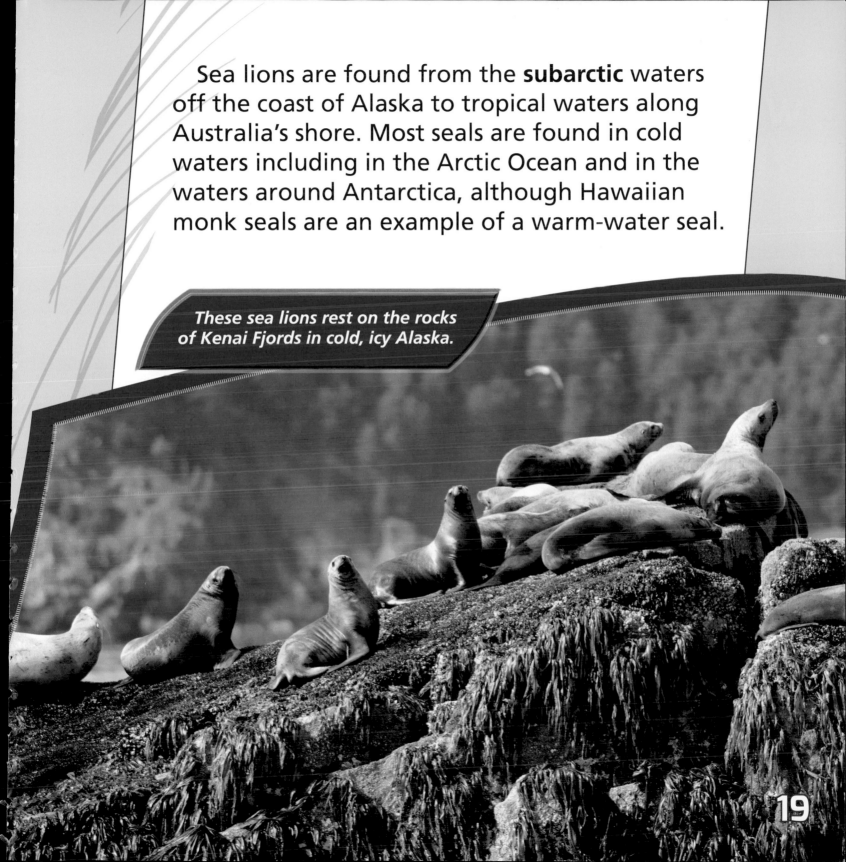

Sea lions are found from the **subarctic** waters off the coast of Alaska to tropical waters along Australia's shore. Most seals are found in cold waters including in the Arctic Ocean and in the waters around Antarctica, although Hawaiian monk seals are an example of a warm-water seal.

These sea lions rest on the rocks of Kenai Fjords in cold, icy Alaska.

WHAT'S UP, PUP?

Male and female pinnipeds come together to **mate** once each year. Males put together a group of females to mate with, called a harem. Many harems may gather in the same place to form a colony. When the mating season becomes birthing season, the colony is called a

This mother seal teaches her pup how to swim and hunt for food in the water.

rookery. These groups of seals or sea lions are social and noisy. They will bark a lot and fight over territory.

Sea lion and seal mothers give birth to a single baby called a pup. A seal or sea lion mother will **nurse** her pup on her rich, fatty milk. In a few weeks, the pup will have put on enough blubber to go into the ocean with its mother and learn to swim and hunt for food.

Galápagos sea lion mothers care for their pups for up to three years, though the pup finds all its own food after about 11 months.

Now you know how to tell the difference between sea lions and seals. You also know how they are alike.

Some species, like California sea lions and harbor seals, are common sights along shorelines. Others, like the Hawaiian monk seal and the Steller sea lion, are

Steller sea lions are the largest of the world's sea lions. They eat mainly fish, squid, and octopuses and are known for forming huge, noisy colonies onshore during breeding season and other times throughout the year.

endangered. Scientists are studying these pinnipeds to understand if their declines are due to habitat loss, climate change, or other reasons. Groups like the World Wildlife Fund work to protect these animals so they will not become **extinct**.

GLOSSARY

adapted (uh-DAPT-ed) Changed to fit requirements.

endangered (in-DAYN-jerd) In danger of no longer existing.

extinct (ik-STINGKT) No longer existing.

insulate (IN-suh-layt) To cover something and stop heat or sound from flowing out of it.

mammals (MA-mulz) Warm-blooded animals that have backbones and hair, breathe air, and feed milk to their young.

mate (MAYT) To come together to make babies.

molt (MOHLT) To shed hair, feathers, shell, horns, or skin.

nurse (NURS) When a female feeds her baby milk from her body.

pinnipeds (PIH-nuh-pedz) A group of animals, which seals belong to, that have flippers instead of legs.

semiaquatic (se-mee-ak-WAH-tik) Lives in water part of the time.

species (SPEE-sheez) One kind of living thing. All people are one species.

subarctic (sub-AHRK-tik) The area just south of the Arctic, which includes much of Alaska, Canada, northern Scandinavia, Siberia, and northern Mongolia.

INDEX

WEBSITES

Due to the changing nature of Internet links, PowerKids Press has developed an online list of websites related to the subject of this book. This site is updated regularly. Please use this link to access the list: www.powerkidslinks.com/hatd/seli/